SEAN SHEPHERD

ribboned / braided / spun

for Harp

HENDON MUSIC

DISTRIBUTED BY

HAL•LEONARD®

7777 W. BLUEMOUND RD. P.O. BOX 13819 MILWAUKEE, WI 53213

www.boosey.com
www.halleonard.com

This work was commissioned by Carnegie Hall.

The World Premiere was given by Sivan Magen
in Weill Recital Hall, Carnegie Hall, New York City on October 21, 2014.

Duration: 10 min.

for Sivan Magen

ribboned / braided / spun
fantasy for harp

SEAN SHEPHERD
(2014)

Elastic and flexible throughout;
♪ = 92-104 / ♩ = 46-52

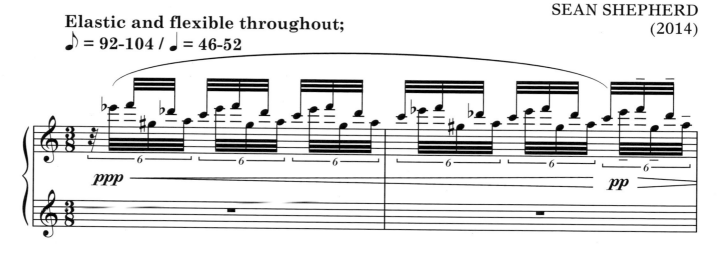

First Printing 2020
Printed in USA

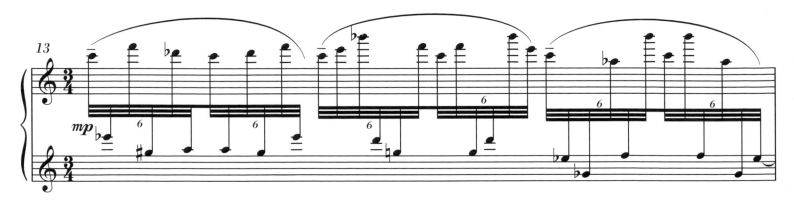

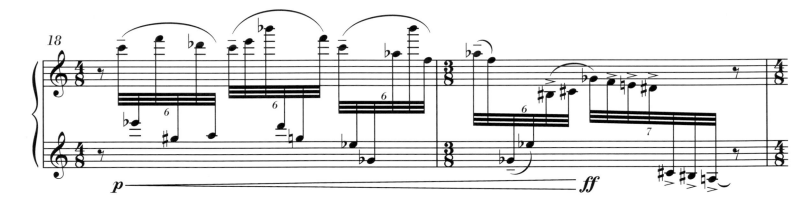

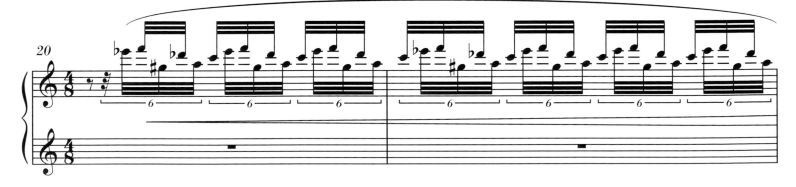

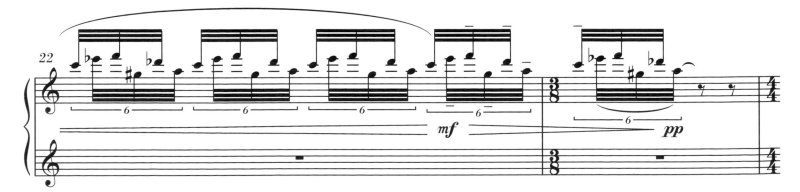

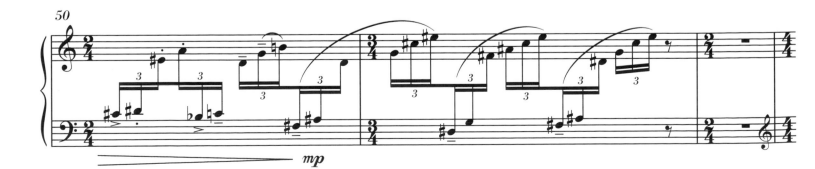

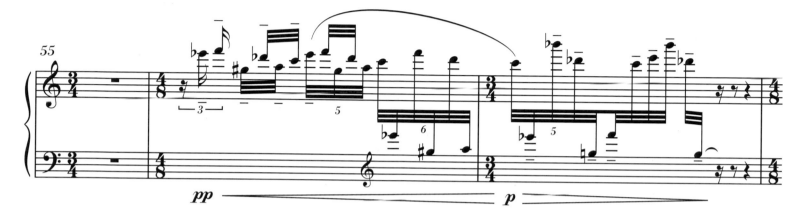

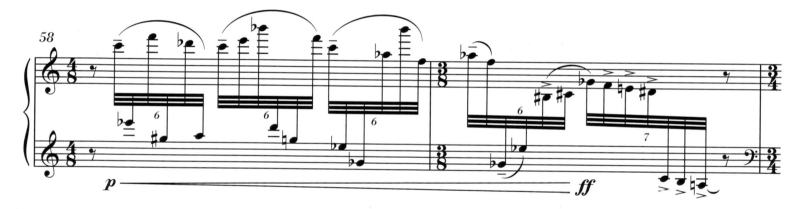

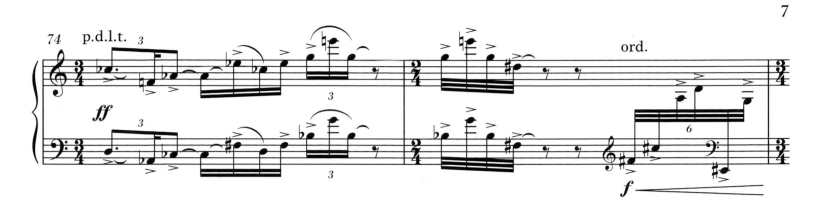

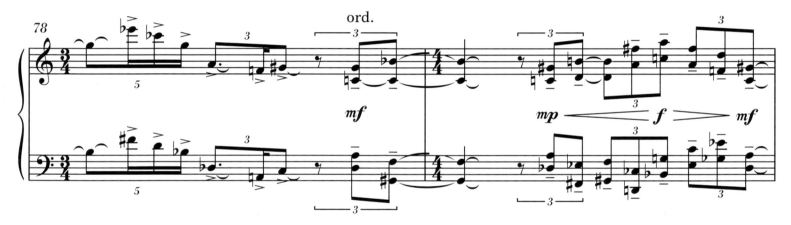

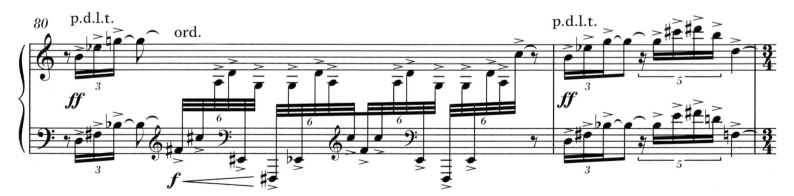

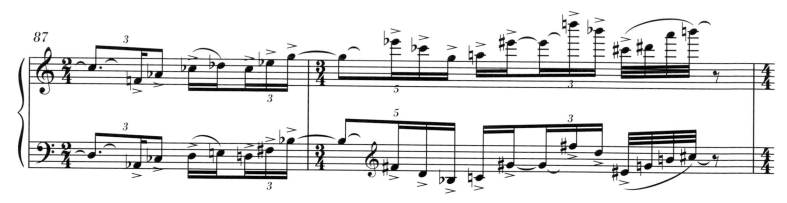

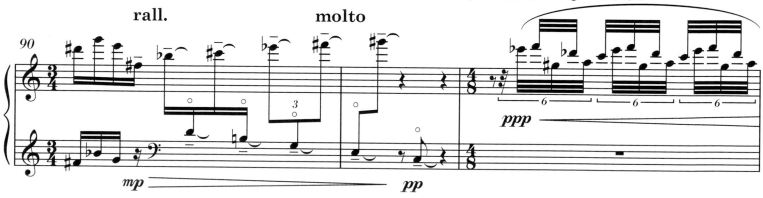

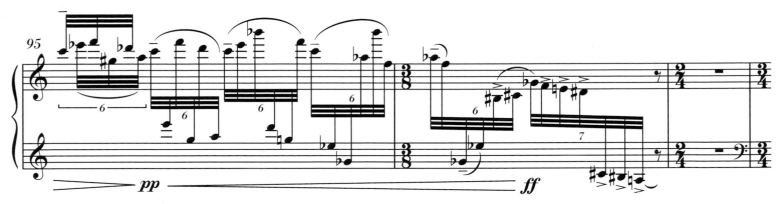

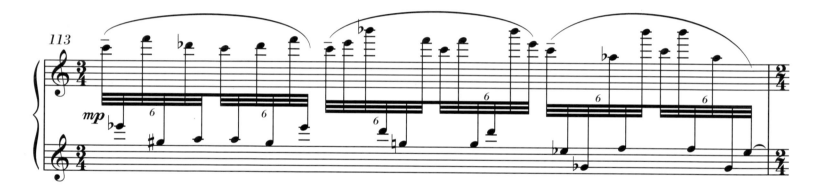

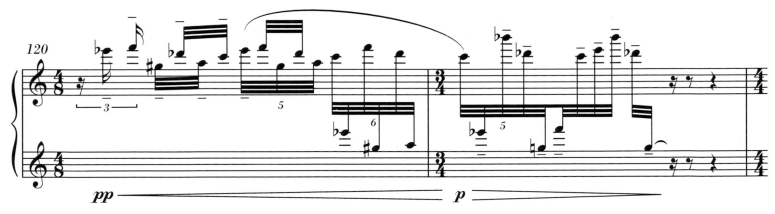

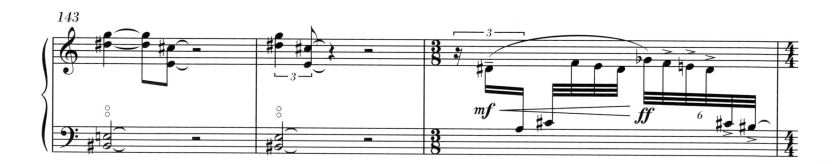